Davand Publishing

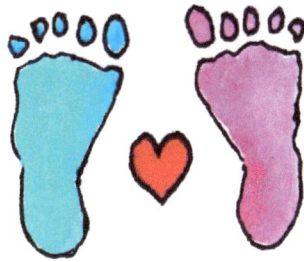

Dedication

In loving memory of the children that inspired this book. They are remembered by thousands by the names of their pages and sites on the internet. I love and miss you all....

Talia Joy Castellano, Ali's Angels, Prayers for Angelina Rose, Kyssi Andrews, Team Franky, Prayers for Makenna Walters, Ambers Awareness for Batten disease, Prayers for Kylie, God's little Warrior, Annie Golden Heart, Faith for Haven Cait, Prayers for Haylee Marie Carl, Charlee's Angels, Addilyn's Journey of Hope, Team Amber, Ezekiel's CDH Journey, Alayna's Journey, Kane's Story: Fighting Batten Disease, Emily's Battle with Batten's Disease, Prayers for Carson, Autumn's Mito Fighting Angels, Love for Laiken and to all those fighting for their lives every day, this is for you.

For a number of years now, I have followed the stories of sick children all over the internet and have prayed for them. I have seen some recover and flourish and sadly, I have seen a number of them die. Some of these children have thousands of followers. I have tried to contact some of these families to offer prayer and my messages have gotten lost in the sea of hundreds, if not thousands of other well-wishers. These caregivers and parents are too busy to answer and wisely don't offer private information or the whereabouts of these children on their public sites.

Because I know that God is still in the healing business and these families need this message, I wrote this simple little healing manual hoping that these books find their way into the hands of those that need it. It is my hope to get these books into every children's hospital or pediatrician's office in the world, but I can't do that alone.

I pray this book is a blessing to you and your loved ones. If you see value in this book and would like to help get copies to families that need it, I ask that you consider giving them to hospitals, nursing homes, doctor's offices or to the sick person down the street. They are available on Amazon.com, Kindle or Createspace. For larger orders, contact me and I'll partner with you for discounts.

Yours In Christ,

Melodie A. Moss

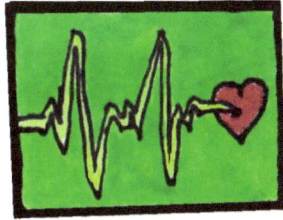

God, Are You There?

Written and Illustrated by Melodie A. Moss

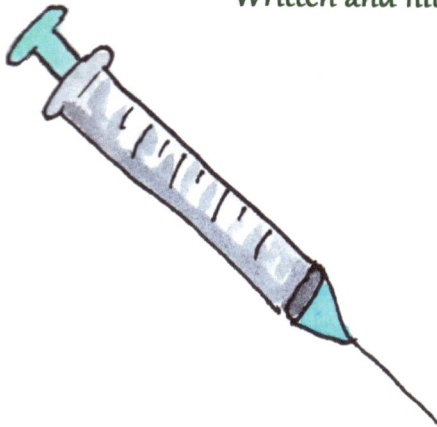

Hello, Darling! I love you.

Sometimes I'm in the hospital and sometimes I'm at home, but no matter where I am, I feel so all alone.

Sometimes I'm in pain and sometimes I feel sick.
I do everything to feel better, but nothing does the trick.

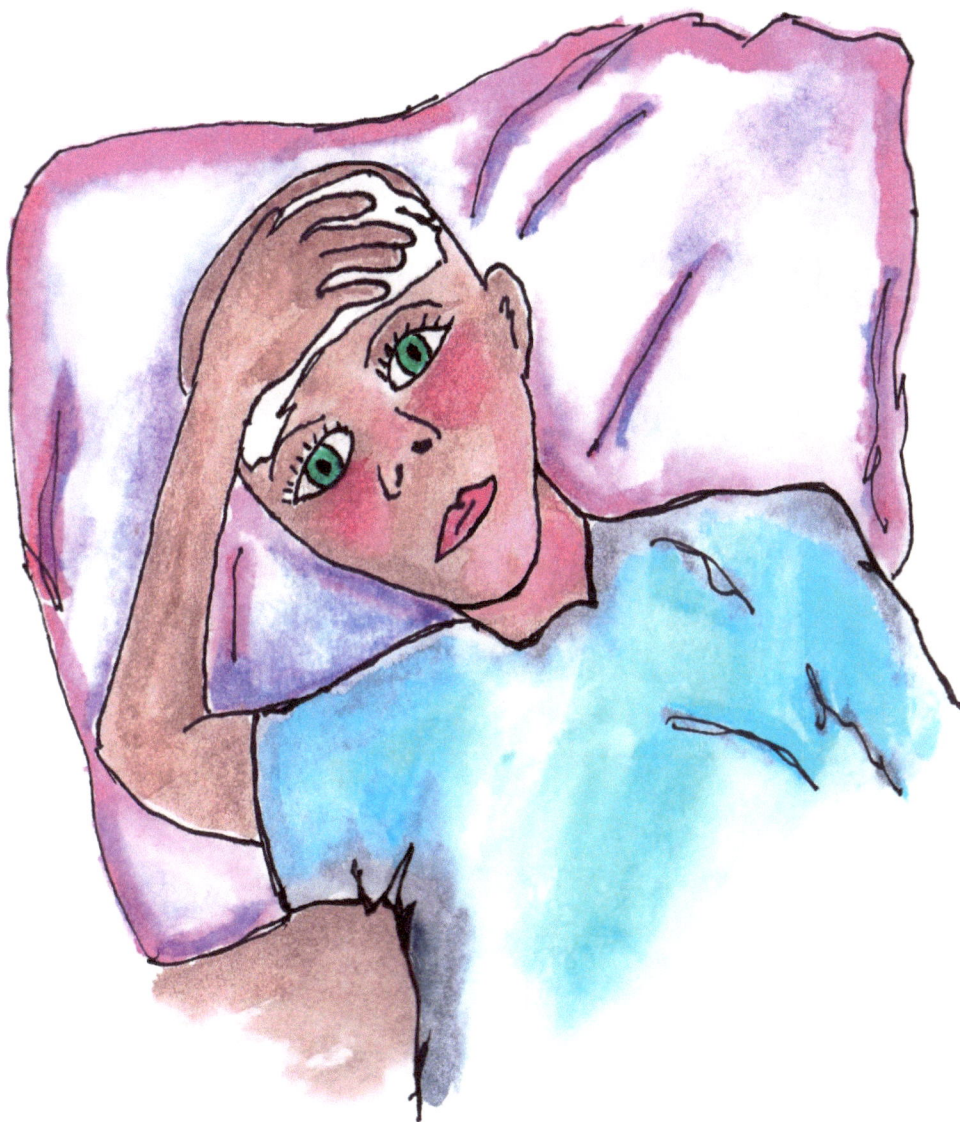

I'm tired of the shots and sick of taking pills.
I'm tired of having a fever and then getting chills.

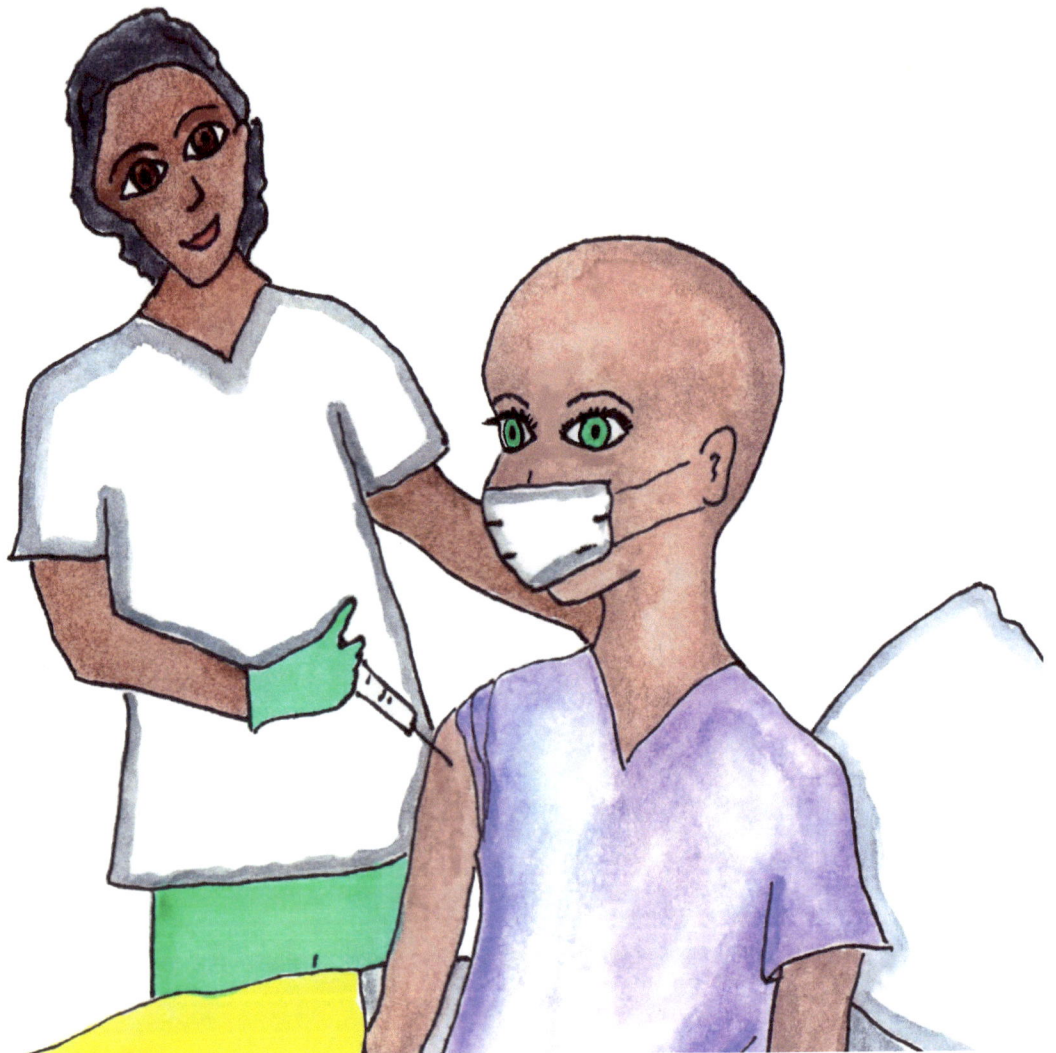

I hate being stuck in bed and that I can't go out and play,
especially when I look outside on a pretty day.

I'm sick of all the tests, but the nurses are sweet.
They help me to a wheelchair and then back on my feet.

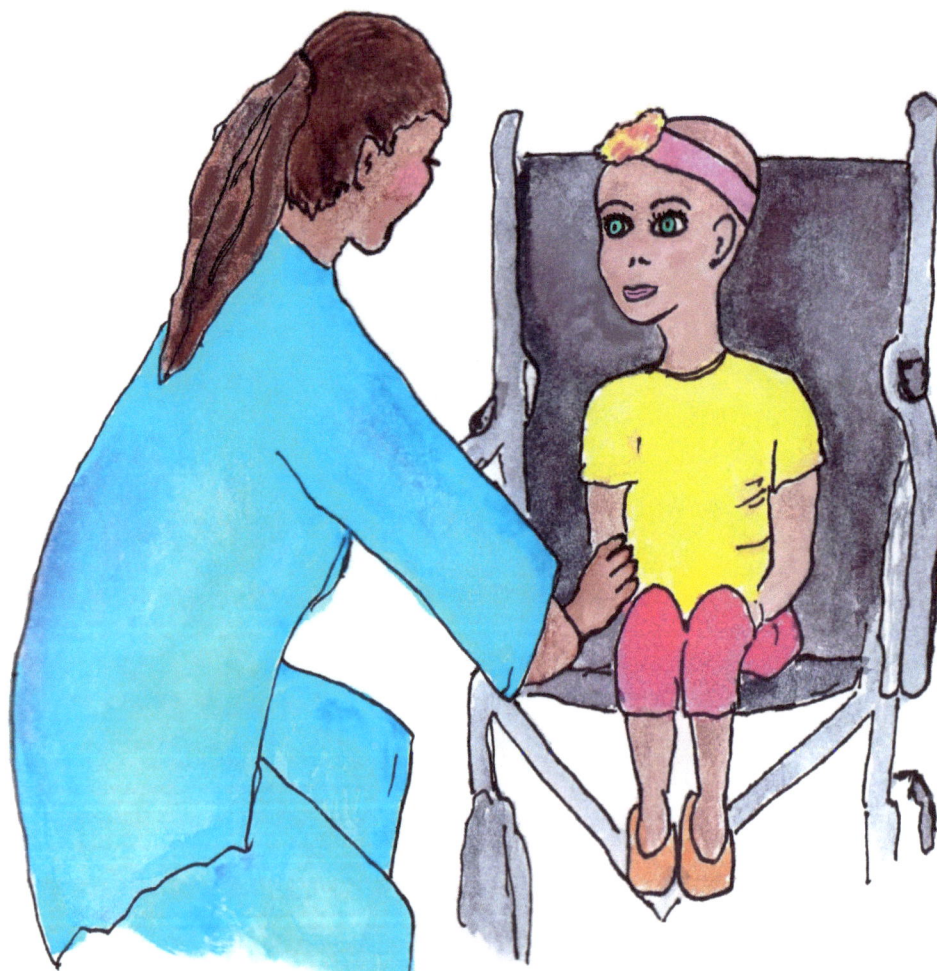

My parents always worry about how much this is gonna cost
and even fight at times 'cause of the job that Mommy lost.

Because I've been sick, I feel that I'm to blame
and I have to wonder if things will ever be the same.

The treatments I take have made me lose my hair
and I have to ask, God, Are You there? Do You care?

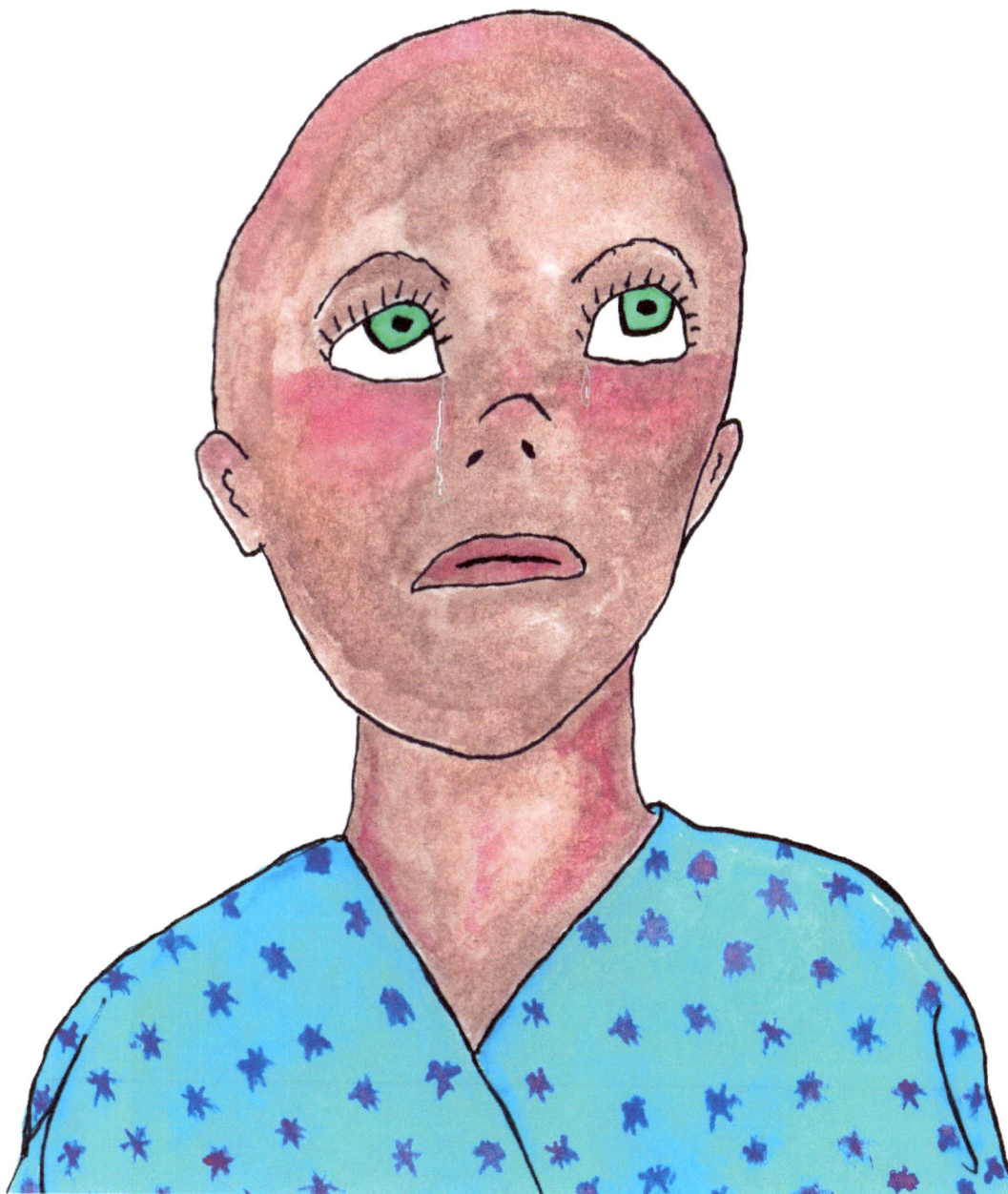

I can't do this anymore and I'm feeling scared and weak.
I can hardly move and can barely even speak.

If You're real, I need some answers 'cause I'm running out of time.
Please help me find You. My life is on the line.

My little one, I've watched and cried and I've seen it all;
your pain, your struggle, and I came when you called.

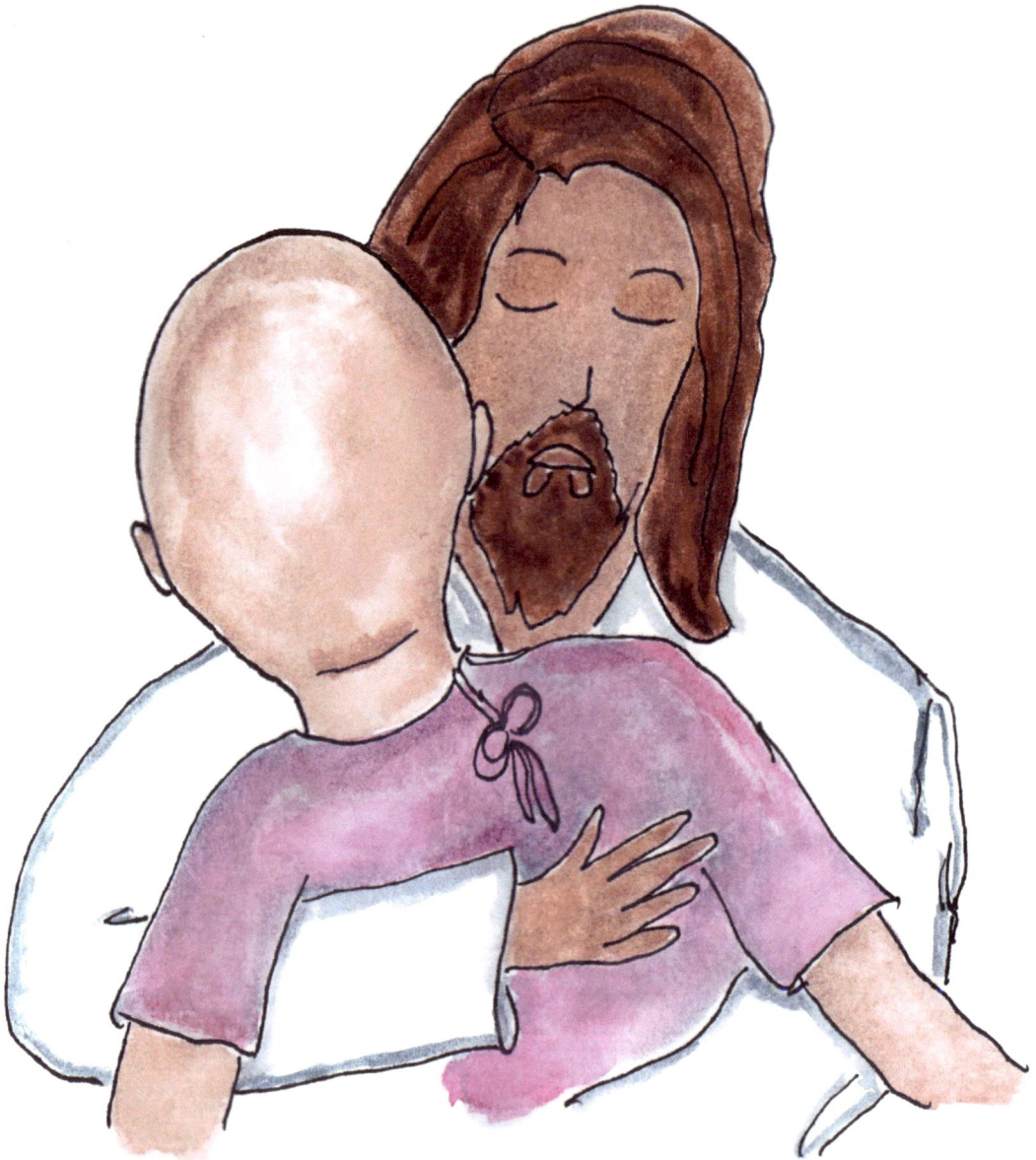

Let Me hold you a bit and kiss away your tears,
put you on My lap and comfort your fears.

You know how much you love your kitten? Well, I love you more.
I've loved you since the day you were born, actually a long time before.

I've healed many that were sick and I'll show you what to do so you can heal yourself and many others too.

Put your hand where you have pain and say, "Pain, you have to go!"
Tell that body part to feel better and believe it will be so.
Any sickness, disease or virus has to go in Jesus name.
I didn't put in on you. The devil is to blame.

Pray over your medicine like you bless your food,
that it not cause you any harm and only do you good.

Keep saying good things about your health and always believe it, that you are getting better and say it until you see it.

If you have a bad day, then find someone else with faith to pray along beside you and in the same way.

Just know even if it might not seem it, you're getting better just the same.
Keep speaking it and believing it and remember to use My Name.

You can heal the sick with the laying on of hands,
at home, or anywhere, even faraway lands.

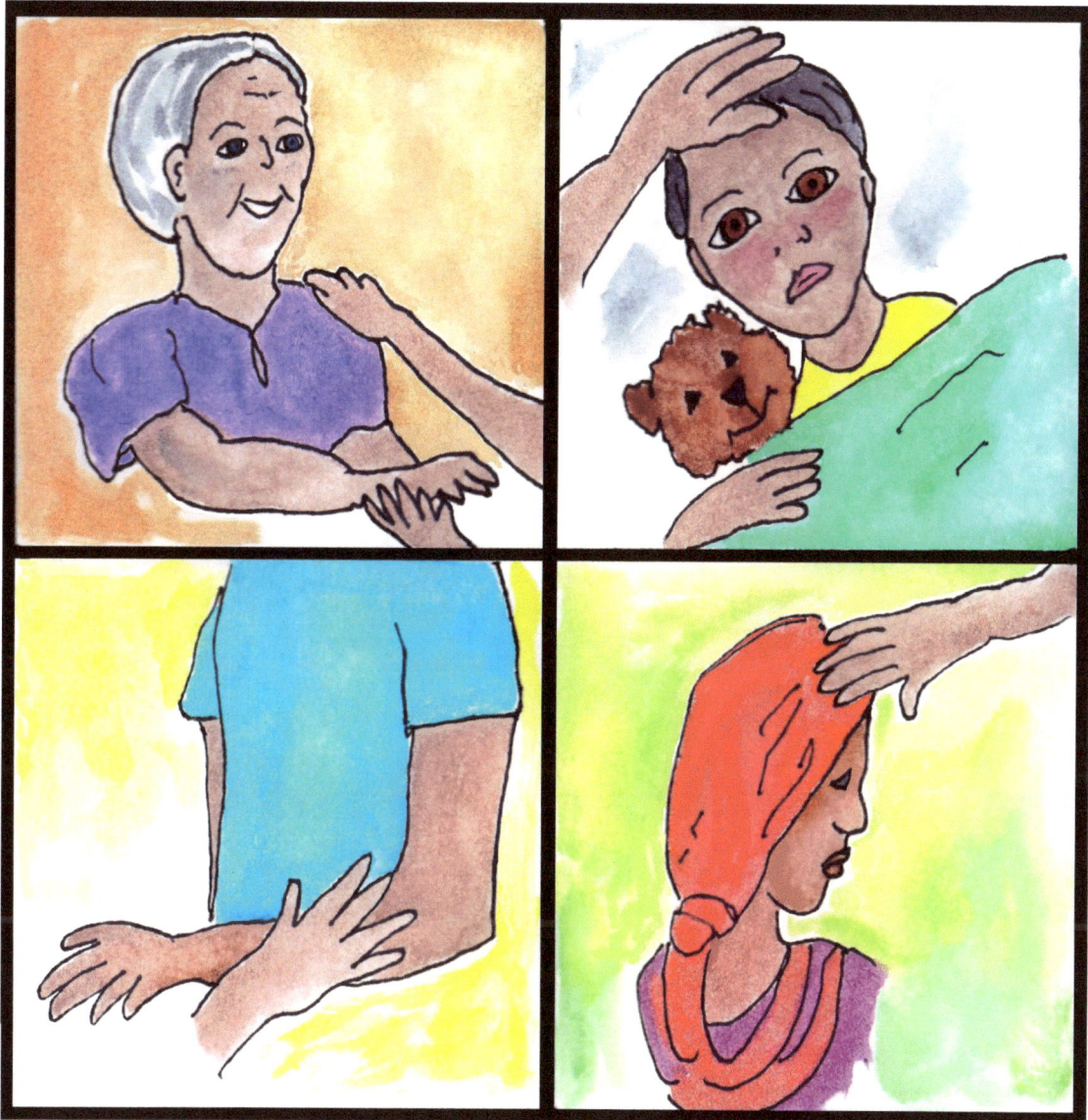

Pray for your parents and for all they have to do.
It's been hard on them, but love will see you through.

Soon you'll feel better and you'll play and run,
dance in the rain and sing in the sun.

Sometimes you'll be happy and sometimes there'll be tears,
but you'll have joy for many, many years.

Know that I am with you in everything you do
and always remember how much that I love you.

Healing Prayer

This book is designed to be a simple healing manual. If you follow what is says to do and believe, you WILL see results. There is no sickness, disease or ailment too big for God. Jesus paid the price for our healing and He deserves what He paid for! The Bible says in John 10:10 that the thief comes to steal, to kill and destroy, but that Jesus came so that we might have life and that more abundantly. If the enemy is trying to steal your life, we have to make him go and he MUST go in the name of Jesus! Below is a sample prayer. If possible, lay hands on the sick person, even yourself, when praying and

ONLY BELIEVE!

In the name of Jesus, I command any sickness, virus, cancer or disease to GO NOW and never return! Death, GO! You are not permitted to steal this life! All pain GO! Any damage from any treatment or medication be reversed now! I speak the Life of God into every cell, system and organ in this body. Thank You Lord for Your healing and for the price You paid for it. The Kingdom of Heaven is at hand! Let it be on earth as it is in heaven now! There is no sickness in heaven and none in this body! Thank you, Lord. Amen!

Father, I join my faith with every reader that applies this prayer in faith and I believe for, not only healing, but for great miracles in their lives in Jesus name, Amen!

Would you like to know my friend, Jesus?

He loves you so much, He even gave His life for you. He wants to be there for you when you're happy or when you're sad. With Him, you'll never be alone. He won't ever leave you or give up on you. He wants you to be happy, healthy and have everything you need. If you'd like a friend like that, just say this little prayer and He will hear you and come to you where you are!

Lord Jesus, I ask that You forgive me of anything bad I've ever done and give me a new start. I believe You came to the world for me, died for me and rose again so I can have a new life too. I ask that You come into my heart and live in me. Teach and guide me all the days of my life and be my friend. Thank You. Amen!

Scriptures

Beloved, I wish above all things that thou mayest prosper and be in health, even as thy soul prospereth.   3 John 2

Who Himself bore our sins in His own body on the tree, that we, having died to sins, might live for righteousness—by whose stripes you were healed.   1 Peter 2:24

And the whole multitude sought to touch Him: for there went virtue out of Him, and healed them all.   Luke 6:19

Now when the sun was setting, all they that had any sick with divers diseases brought them unto Him; and He laid His hands on every one of them, and healed them.   Luke 4:40

But when Jesus knew it, He withdrew himself from thence: and great multitudes followed Him, and He healed them all.
Matthew 12:15

 And these signs shall follow them that believe; In My Name shall they cast out devils; they shall speak with new tongues; They shall take up serpents; and if they drink any deadly thing, it shall not hurt them; they shall lay hands on the sick, and they shall recover.
Matthew 16:17-18

Jesus said unto him, If thou canst believe, all things are possible to him that believeth.   Mark 9:23

Scriptures

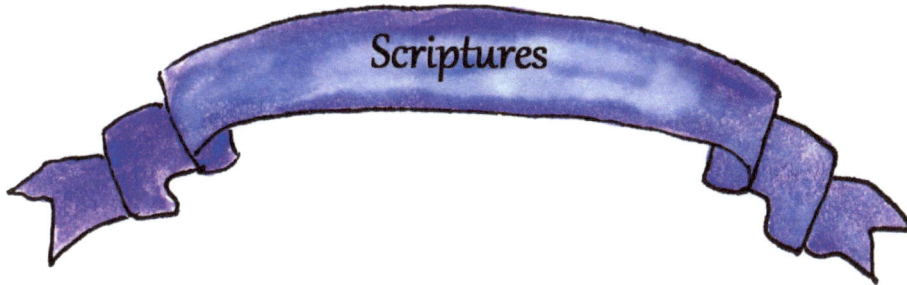

For verily I say unto you, That whosoever shall say unto this mountain, Be thou removed, and be thou cast into the sea; and shall not doubt in his heart, but shall believe that those things which he saith shall come to pass; he shall have whatsoever he saith. Therefore I say unto you, What things soever ye desire, when ye pray, believe that ye receive them, and ye shall have them.   Mark 11:23-24

And whatsoever ye shall ask in My Name, that will I do, that the Father may be glorified in the Son. If ye shall ask any thing in My Name, I will do it.   John 14:13-14

And as ye go, preach, saying, The kingdom of heaven is at hand.
Heal the sick, cleanse the lepers, raise the dead, cast out devils: freely ye have received, freely give.   Matthew 10:7-8

O Lord my God, I cried unto thee, and thou hast healed me. Psalm 30:2

But he was wounded for our transgressions, he was bruised for our iniquities: the chastisement of our peace was upon him; and with his stripes we are healed.   Isaiah 53:5

He healeth the broken in heart, and bindeth up their wounds. Psalm 147:3

www.ingramcontent.com/pod-product-compliance
Lightning Source LLC
Chambersburg PA
CBHW041238040426
42445CB00004B/75